lavish lines/luscious lies

Saadia Ali Aschemann

ISBN -13 978-0-9774126-2-4

Library of Congress Control Number: 2007925746

Photography by Chet Coonrod of Coonrod Photography

Published by FireFly Publishing & Entertainment

Printed in the United States by Morris Publishing
3212 East Highway 30
Kearney, NE 68847
1-800-650-7888

This book is dedicated to my sons, Noah and Davis, who are a source of constant inspiration.

Overserved: A Rondeau

Always overserved, dizziness undeserved
My empty glass forever observed
I refuse to take the blame
for my tipsy acclaim
Can my sobriety ever be preserved?

Good wine should be conserved
inebriation reserved
Heavy handed waiters have no shame
always overserved

Wine wielding traitors leave me unnerved
with twisted motives--curved
Contributing to my Chardonnay fame
Unfilled goblets call their name
balance swerved
always overserved

***A lyrical poem of French origin having between 13 and 15
lines with two rhymes throughout and with the first half of**

the first line repeated twice as a refrain. The rhyme scheme is typically aabba, aabR, aabbaR in a rondeau.

Migraine

Behind my eyes
a little boy
kicks
his heavy shoes
against my brain

Fat, angry fists
pound
my sinuses

Screaming synapses
Arguing axons

Mutiny, my cranium cracks

Tantrums and discontent
echo
inside my head

Jack Daniels

Jack hurts
makes me cry
He alerts
passers-by
To my every flaw
exposure
I am raw
he is secure
With his power
knows only strength
At this late hour
sees the length
That I'll travel
for oblivion and escape
Laughing as I unravel
Jack rapes
I despise him
he hates me
Forever
Sworn enemies

Wordplay

To covet is covert
An alarm--an alert
Want is sometimes wanton
To connive--a con
Mysterious mistress
Assesses assets
Caress and confess
This sweet sweat
Marvelous, I marvel
Excellence excels
Here lives a heretic
My fantasy fantastic

Kyrielle

God have mercy on my soul
Behavior that I can't control
Violating my probation
Resisting anything but temptation

Deliverance so dull
Nobility's appeal null
Ignoring promises of salvation
Resisting anything but temptation

Of my questionable deeds
I need no confirmation
My shadow self feeds
Resisting anything but temptation

Demons adore
My deviation
Too entertained to abhor
Resisting anything but temptation

Reality borne of my imagination
Resisting anything but temptation

My realization
Resisting anything but temptation

*the name and character of the *'kyrielle'* come from the Catholic Mass, whose wail of *Kyrie eleison!*--'Lord, have

mercy upon us'--is a familiar refrain. The final line of every stanza is the same. There is no set length and both quatrains and couplets may be used.

Inspired by R. Frost

fiery desire
cold hate
seems somewhat extreme
unrealistic--a dictate

what about slouching toward nirvana
or lukewarm interest
tell me the temperature
of a forbidden request

must we burn
or freeze
forgetting the delight
of a breezy tease

perhaps sadness should boil
oblivion could be mild
survival of the fittest
feelings gone wild

Unfinished

he is a sealed envelope	an unwritten story	a locked vault
addressed to someone else	that begs to be told	promising treasure to key holders
that i can not open		inaccessible

unexpressed ideas	an unconsummated	unfinished business
that float in literary purgatory	rendezvous	loose ends, wanting
	closure	
	buzzing with tension	

his mind:
like a house with
a thousand windows
he slips away
easily, undetected
sitting outside of his isolated genius
hoping for admission
i wait patiently

Note to reader: try reading this poem vertically and horizontally.

Request

Meet me, the text reads
and I want to speed through time and space
My skin pleads
needs
his dark embrace

Meet me, he asks
and I feel so ready
For his tasks
he unmasks
remembering makes me unsteady

Meet me, the message says
and I envision locks
black and gray
someday
Actuality mocks

Meet him?
Only behind sleepy lids
My familiar stranger

danger
Our kisses hid

Wedding Night Pantoum*

Wrapping myself in a single sheet
In room 521 at The Ritz
I can hear my heart beat
My questions quit

In room 521 at The Ritz
Whispers burn
My questions quit
He helps me learn

Whispers burn
Room service brings more wine
He helps me learn
Replaces the privacy sign

Room service brings more wine
He plays with my hair
Replaces the privacy sign
Our luxurious lair

He plays with my hair
I can hear my heart beat

Our luxurious lair
Wrapping myself in a single sheet

*A pantoum is a strict, 15th century form of poetry that must be composed in full cross rhymed quatrains (abab, cdcd, etc.). It must begin and end with the same line, and this is how the rest of the poem unfolds: the 2nd and 4th lines of the first stanza become the 1st and 3rd lines of the second stanza, the 2nd and 4th lines of the second stanza become the 1st and 3rd of stanza three and so on until you reach the end. A pantoum may be as long or short as you desire, but, when you do get to the end, you must use the two lines you will not yet have repeated--the 1st and 3rd of the opening stanza, they are reversed in order and become the 2nd and 4th of the final quatrain. The next two poems, 'Solitude' and 'February' are also classic pantoums. Surprisingly, the poem entitled 'Persuasion' is technically a pantoum, though it is not a classic example because each line is only composed of one word.

Solitude

Alone
In this suite
Whereabouts unknown
Solitude—a treat

In this suite
At the Ritz
Solitude—a treat
My skin moonlit

At the Ritz
Rocky Balboa on demand
My skin moonlit
Wine on the nightstand

Rocky Balboa on demand
Lounging, languid
Wine on the nightstand
So heavy, my eyelids

Lounging, languid
Whereabouts unknown
So heavy, my eyelids
Alone

February

You give off such heat, he writes
His words feel delicious
Email that ignites
My want is vicious

His words are delicious
Missives both solid and airy
My want is vicious
Sign of the times--my February

Missives both solid and airy
I giggle at his desires
Sign of the times--my February
Adoring the way he admires

I giggle at his desires
He asks to kiss my neck
Adoring the way he admires
Have I melted? I check

He asks to kiss my neck

Awakening with a double click

Have I melted? I check

Messages erotic

Awakening with a double click

Email that ignites

Messages erotic

You give off such heat, he writes

<u>Persuasion</u>

smile
laugh
touch
flirt

laugh
wink
flirt
kiss

wink
tease
kiss
please

tease
touch
please
smile

Paradox

She confuses
Callous, easily bruises

Our girl is nothing
If not a contradiction

Left and right wing
Unsure conviction

Silk peignoirs
Smoking cigars

X rated texts
During PTA meetings

Vexed
Still laughing at everything

Tattooed ass
Flying first class

Collecting firearms
Wearing good jewelry to box

Her smile disarms
Sacrilegious orthodox

Oxymoron personified
Insecure, satisfied

New Years Day

Stirring my bloody mary
With a thick stalk
Of celery
I make breakfast for my family
Muffins and eggs
My diet forsaken

My oldest son demands bacon
Asking for a sip of my bloody mary
My youngest holds on to my leg
My husband and I talk
Resolutions expressed shyly
Pretty lies our commentary

Our guarantees
Awaken
Frozen dreams, chilly
Our life on this prairie
Solid as rock
Different as nutmeg

Why renege?
With an existence so very
Secure...a lock
I sprinkle some cayenne
In my bloody mary
I need some more vodka really

My drink makes me silly
I nibble on eggs
Sip my disappearing mary
A new years query
Leaves me taken
Too much double talk

I'd like to take a walk
Our whole family
It's too cold--godforsaken
My baby still holds onto my leg
Suburban scenery
This moment legendary

Barbie

He wants a barbie doll
Simple, uncomplicated
A house cat--domesticated
          Available for his call

I was raised to please
Grimacing through bikini waxes
Paying kept woman taxes
          His desire appeased

He hates chipped polish
Ponytails and baby fat
Late dinners, girly chit chat
          I grant his wish

He asks so much
Refusing imperfection
Quick with rejection
          My blemishes, I retouch

Note to reader: I used an *abba* rhyming scheme for this particular poem, often called an 'envelope rhyme.'

History: A Terza Rima

Old boyfriends haunt
Like freaky ghosts
My memories taunt

Forgotten--almost
A long ago love note
Sent by post

They promote
Polluting my atmosphere
With smoggy anecdotes

Shadows made clear
Bittersweet
Attempting to endear

I remember heat
Long legged effect
Kisses and deceit

Is my life perfect
They always ask
Questions that infect

I now wear a mask
Hiding truth
My responsible task

Invincible youth
The girl I was

Long ago truth
Together just because

*An open stanzaic form with interlocking cross-rhyming.
The middle line of each stanza forms the outer rhymes of
the next stanza. When the writer comes to the end of the
poem, a fourth line is added to the last stanza to use up the
rhyme that would have otherwise gone to the next. This
form was used by Dante in his *Inferno*. The following poem
'Hush' is also an example of a terza rima.

<u>Hush</u>

:::read in a whisper:::

not dirty, hardly clean
my secret
somewhere in between

a confirmed threat
difficult to admit
dangerous...and yet

impossible to quit
detox would be brutal
my loyalties split

to deny myself--futile
why suffer?
playing femme fatale

harder, rougher
I prefer
arduous and tougher

my readers concur
what a rush
don't forget to whisper
my secret—hush

Innuendo

he insinuates
with his smile
his suggestion permeates
my denial
primitive affinity
nuclear attraction
me, myself and I...the trinity
fleeting satisfaction
my idea pleases
he unzips my skin
his whisper teases
I let him in

Guinness

Dark as a starless night
Just as unexpected
A pint of Guinness is a delight
My muse and I--connected

Irish stout
Fantastic
No doubt
Drastic

The drink has bite
A rough lover
Don't fight
Discover

Guinness is freedom
Release
From who I've become
Peace

On my 35th Birthday*

I paint my lips
with raspberry gloss
The tint is luscious and I
think about

boys
enjoyed   kissed
music   children
read   born
books   wine
tasted
friends made

I can m
e
a
s
u
r
e my life
in these
m
o
m
e
n
t
s

***this is an example of concrete poetry. This type of poetry
visually conveys the poet's meaning through the graphic**

arrangement of letters, words, or symbols on the page. For instance, the above poem is written like sand falling through an hourglass.

Girl/Crack

Broken girl cracked in half
Not the full story--a paragraph

Public face free of flaws
Frozen princess before the thaw

Her smile--home
Her laugh a poem

Reconciliation of such different sides
Could perfection and alter egos coincide?

Questionable thoughts, fertile mind
Locked up and confined

Secrets and wandering eyes
Hidden under an immaculate disguise

Earthquake
Soul ache

A cracked girl resonates wide and far
Fascination lies in the bizarre

Word Association

Error: human

Forgive: divine

Secret: delicious

Stars: align

Affair: remember

Seduction: wine

Yes: more

Strength: spine

Tryst: luxury

Rise: shine

Ravenous: you

Together: fine

<u>Sonic Repetition*</u>

Tip it back
Eat prozac
Try to attract
Say no to crack
Give feedback
Follow the pack
Leave Iraq
Cut some slack
Use Kodak
Bet offtrack
Shop Frontenac
Talk some smack
Drink cognac
Paint it black
Own your mack
Don't be wack
Just the facts
Have my back?
Hit the sack

*sonic repetition is the repetition of sounds in a poem

Manicures

Men are like
manicures

Never perfect for long

Chips and cracks
appear at the first hint
of duress

The bolder the hue
the more glaring the imperfection

Ragged truth
hiding under glossy lacquer

Like manicures,
men are ready
for replacement
or change
After a few short days

Sestina*

I told him I was writing a sestina
He said it sounded like a drink
Laughing, I thought of a poetic cocktail
And drinkable words
If only I could inhabit such a world
I live for these dreams

Poetry and letters bounce around my dreams
Something as intricate as a sestina
In a convenience worshipping world
Might be easier if I fix myself a drink
A pretty, potent cocktail
Adult beverages help my words

Powerful--the wonder of words
Provocative, tempting, spinning dreams
Thoughts and words swim in my cocktail
The drink emboldens--maybe I'll finish this sestina
Let me take a sip, a drink
I am suddenly sure, the master of my world

My corner of the world
Furnished with inspiration and words
I decorate with a drink
My indulgences fuel my dreams
Tonight, in my sleep, I'll envision a finished sestina
As I sip a dreamy cocktail

Why is it so important--the cocktail?
Libations are necessary in my world

They help my mind grind out a sestina
They bring interest to my words
Wine gives good dreams
I shouldn't admit it, but I adore the drink

Any drink
Or, should I say, any cocktail
Gives me unattainable dreams
About a Utopian world
Where girls like me can get lost in words
Endlessly working on a sestina

A drink is an escape in our manic world
Written words are more delicious with a cocktail
I drift off toward my dreams, thinking about my sestina

*The sestina is an old fixed form of poetry, dating as far back as the twelfth century. It consists of six six-line stanzas and a three-line concluding stanza, called an envoi. The ending words of the first stanza are repeated throughout each subsequent stanza in a set pattern. So, in this particular sestina, the words that I repeat are: *sestina, drink, cocktail, words, world and dreams*. The numeric formula for the poem is 6-1-5-2-4-3, meaning the sixth line of the previous stanza would be line number 1 in the next, the first line of the previous stanza would be the second line and so on. The same six words appear in the concluding three-line stanza, two in each line.

Drunken Dreams

Too many libations
Turn my dreams into sensations

School busses collide with giant toothbrushes
I see fountains from which mac and cheese rushes

Whether it's Chardonnay or Beefeater, rocks...
Drunken dreams knock off my socks

I wake up shivering and smiling at the same time
Should drinking and dreaming be considered a crime?

Booze helps give my dreams voice
Sobriety or inebriation--it really isn't a choice

I love the movies that play in my mind
I watch them once, then press rewind

Allegory

It's like this:
when I reminisce
at the edge of the abyss
my memories—hard to dismiss

I remember what I was drinking
more than what I was thinking

Nights with Cristal, nights with Jack
befriending Tom Collins and cognac

Flirting with princes and kingmakers
street sweepers and heartbreakers

Forever finding solace in my drink
the missing link

Contentment can be poured
a smorgasbord

Of liquid selections

drinkable perfection

A cocktail laboratory
my tipple territory
fluid memory
allegory

Johnnie Walker Black: A Rubai

Johnnie makes me mean
A bitchy queen
Vicious in public
An open flame licking gasoline

Speaking my mind
Unfortunately unkind
My words hurt
Delivered, sealed and signed

I like him straight
Cornering fate
Good behavior makes dull memories
Wicked times await

Scotch whiskey works quickly
Few would disagree
Johnnie does his job well
Setting drinkers free

He does not lie
No need to falsify

The truth lives in every bottle
To this, I testify

*Ruba'iyat or rubaiyat (Arabic: رباعیات) (a plural word derived from the root meaning 'four') means "quatrains" in the Persian language. Singular: ruba'i (rubai, ruba'ee, rubayi, rubayee). The rhyme scheme is AABA, i.e., lines 1, 2 and 4 rhyme.

This verse form was popularized in Edward FitzGerald's translation of the collection of Persian verses known as the Rubaiyat of Omar Khayyam. In fact, Rubaiyat is a common shorthand name for this collection.

Enigma

Afterwards, I feel electric
An eccentric heretic
Erotic
Even tantric

I remember his voice
My decision, my choice
Sweetheart, he chants, bi-coastal brilliance
Dependent on my nonchalance
Texts that read ready
Make me instantly heady
Heated
My inhibitions deleted
Unfamiliar, foreign
Cellular Superman
Would his touch be as infernal?
Branding flesh--clues external

He releases me always
Without a gaze

Untitled

i like pretty lies
more than ugly truths
deception can be satisfying
i can be
young
beautiful and
desirable
forever
so
lie to me
baby

Sleepwalker

I sleepwalk
At all hours
A model on a catwalk
My submission empowers

A sleep voyager
Navigating furniture and carpet
A drowsy provocateur
Grace and oblivion: a duet

Confident in my travels
Hip swinging, he tells me, *so fine*
Fluid, composed by Ravel
Operating in slumber--divine

I wake in different rooms
Coming to, enveloped in confusion
Trying not to assume
That daybreak is an intrusion

My nocturnal wandering

My nighttime journey
Risking everything
For my moment of free

Triolet*

Lending sex to any occasion
Leather pants are not shy
Never bashful, always brazen
Lending sex to any occasion
A slippery invasion
No matter the location
Lending sex to any occasion
Leather pants are not shy

*A poem or stanza of eight lines with a rhyme scheme abaaabab, in which the fourth and seventh lines are the same as the first, and the eighth line is the same as the second.

Another example of a triolet is below:

Don't Lie

He wants to hit it and quit it
Of this, I have no doubt
I'm accepting—he should admit
He wants to hit it and quit it
Deception is lame, counterfeit
I'm not asking for a handout
He wants to hit it and quit it
Of this I have no doubt

Dirty Martini

Extra olive juice
Makes the drink dirty
My excuse
For being extra flirty

A dirty martini
Simple and complicated
A bikini
Its appeal calculated

Shaken or stirred
Is irrelevant
Dirty is preferred
My experiment

A researcher charting
Cause and effect
Control and sobriety parting
The buzz perfect

How many sips
Does it take

For an eclipse
My shadow self wakes

SAHM*: Anapest Monometer**

Pick that up!
Is this fun?
Are you done?
Don't be rude!
Peas are good.
Yes, you should.
I love you!
Can you smile?
Wait a while.
Be happy!
Go to sleep!
Not a peep!
Stop right now.
Get in bed.
Watch your head!
Dad is home!
Where are you?
Peek a boo!
Brush your teeth.
Let me see.
One, two, three...
I'm counting
Don't you tease.
Kisses please!
Clean your room!
Be polite.
Nighty night!

*Stay At Home Mom

**Anapest is a meter having two unstressed syllables followed by a stressed syllable. For example: (− − /). Monometer is a verse written in one foot lines. So, for instance if the line would read "Pick that up is this fun" that would be a line composed of two feet.

Game Recognizes Game

Recognition
Is sometimes intuition
Sudden intimacy, instant friendship
Like watching a filmstrip
That you've seen before
Not a whisper, but a roar
Immediate understanding
Connection, commanding
I know you said silently
Flaws overlooked gently
Allegiance right away
Raw like doomsday
Respect
The subject

3 Haiku*

Written after reading Ginsberg

haikus kick my ass
more syllables are needed
to express myself

five-seven-five is
not adequate to explain
mystery, beauty

my thoughts are never
sparse or tight or efficient
my words need freedom

*A Japanese lyric verse form having three unrhymed lines of 5, 7 and 5 syllables, traditionally invoking an aspect of nature or the seasons.

Four Tanka*

his benediction
a sinful want, answered prayer
spices—like cayenne
rush through her capillaries
two sides…Madonna and whore

an elegant freak
a luxurious present
begs to be unwrapped
raw inside, ready, willing
to make dreams come true for him

she accepts mistakes
respects infidelity
a contradiction
honors technicalities
only wanting to please him

feminine mystique
so uncool she burns it up
feminists nightmare
she's her own inspiration
forever stands by her man

*Tanka, like haiku, is another Japanese form consisting of five lines of 5-7-5-7-7 syllables, respectively.

Curses

Written after reading Bukowski

I swear
Like a motherfucker
Dropping words without fanfare
Similar to a crass trucker

Lost in the labyrinth of highways
Who hasn't been home in days
I use colorful language like punctuation
Commas, periods and exclamations

The fiery orange of fuck, the watery blue of damn
Is as pleasing as a hologram

To hear me curse: surprising
Incongruity is appetizing

The sacred does not exist without the profane
Pleasure is useless without the pain

Son of a Bitch, my glossy mouth growls
There is comfort in insanity
Language that is foul
Defines my vanity

Baby's Breath

The flowers he sent me
were full of baby's breath
Dry and white
their name seemed wrong
My baby's breath
is not light, or airy
His breath
is hot and lusty
Fiery
a steam engine
Solid
like legos
Far from weak
or wispy
His little boy chest
rises and falls
Strong breath
even and determined
So different from
a papery flower

103 Degrees

Damn.
This fever
      has made me a believer
I offer medicated prayers and
             heated vows
I fight infection
        like a warrior
            with prescriptions and potions
             murdering infiltrates
      before they acclimate
to my boiling blood
Restless
      an evicted fish
          searching for water
    I burn
Infernal
    on fire, internal
Hallucinating
    Liquidating
My skin melts

Rhyme Royal*

to be read while being beautiful

beauty is currency
honored everywhere
beauty--a master key
unlocking with pretty hair
her power is unfair
like new money flaunting big bills
real beauty takes little skill

a cross and a commodity
beauty dares
admirers to disagree
to disregard the blare
of her white hot glare
Burning but chill
beautiful girls fulfill

*This poem is an example of Rhyme Royal. This type of rhyme is associated with Geoffrey Chaucer, whose *Troilus and Criseyde* marks the form's first appearance in English. Basically, it is a seven line stanza with an ababbcc rhyme scheme. If I were really following the rules, each line would have been written in iambic pentameter. However, being the rule breaker that I am, each line has a meter all its own.

Before

Before
he comes home
I

get off the phone
toss the salad
pour some wine
empty my mind
clear the dishwasher
pour some more wine
                    (this Chardonnay is delicious)
dust the children
kiss the furniture
cook the laundry
wash the pasta
floss my makeup
fix my teeth

pour some more music
and
listen to Chardonnay

Text

he gives good text
his words--tropic
midday on an uncrowded island
looking for a drink
his texts, that hot

my reaction--reflex
shortsighted and myopic
this unexplored land
on the brink
of a forgotten memory. A snapshot.

our distance leaves me vexed
a little heartsick
my phone chimes and
vibrates--a cellular wink
ignore him? i can not.

morse code, these texts
a new millennium trick
for my exile--inland
removed and out of sync
an escape? i plot.

What comes next
an unfortunate click
powered off--missives banned
that fidelity kink
to surrender? i fought.

Ars Poetica*

I can't help it
I like my poems to rhyme
Do you hate me?
              I hear you
                 Louder and <u>**clearer**</u>
              Than my own voice
You think I'm hopelessly uncool
                 (I know I am)
I need to be more avant garde
                 (This is true)
I'm not edgy enough
                 (Yes)

I wish I could string mismatched
                     words together with
                 careless brilliance
                 without rhyme, though,
              my words seem incomplete
                 half written
like a child's wish list
an unfinished argument
                 waiting for closure

Or maybe not

I have to make sure my shit's backed up
                 giddyup
I couldn't resist
                 <u>**my rhymes exist**</u>

*A poem praising poetry or written about poetry, or even about the poem a poet is writing at the moment.

Chardonnay

The color of liquid gold
Appealing as a centerfold

Just as forward and full bodied
Drinkable food, mind feed

A sip starts the vehicle
Promising a tipsy tickle

Manicured nails tap at the crystal stem
Waiting to invoke mayhem

The finish chills
Thrills

Is bracing
Self-effacing

Empty bottles line up like soldiers--front line
Thinking of days past, white roses and wine

Sandwiches

I promise to cut the crusts off

their grilled cheese sandwiches
The stove sizzles and my
children
kick a soccer ball towards me as I
pour juice and listen
to little boy laughs
We discuss the superiority of
The Incredible Hulk and build
architecturally sound Lego towers
I create a maze of railroad tracks that
Thomas the Tank Engine can navigate and
the three of us play
Mario Kart while we nibble on
warm, toasted cheese sandwiches
with

the crusts cut off

My Muse: Anaphora*

She is a needy infant

She is a stubborn toddler

She is a petulant child

She holds her breath

She refuses to talk to me

She shuts me out

She demands constant stimulation

She speaks in languages that I don't understand

She is thirstier than a desperate housewife or a shy guest

She holds me hostage in my own house and insists   .

       on expensive wine and my isolation before she
will come out and play

***Anaphora is a fancy poetic term for when the beginning of
each line in a poem repeats the same word or phrase. In the
above poem, the repetition of the pronoun, 'she', at the
beginning of each line, forces the reader to pay attention to
the qualities of my muse and the way I struggle with 'her.'
The repetition suggests obsession, and, certainly obsession
is a part of my poetic journey. The variation at the end is**

meant to show that sometimes I do break free of her (my muse's) infinite requests, or perhaps that my obsession, poetry, can leave me alone once in a while.

The next poem is also an example of anaphora. Again, obsession is suggested with the repetition of the words 'pretty baby.' This particular poem does not break up the repetition at the end—leading the reader to believe that the relationship is still very one sided.

Pretty Baby

Written after reading Ginsberg

pretty baby he says

pretty baby he breathes

pretty baby come here

pretty baby don't leave

pretty baby show me

pretty baby I need

pretty baby say yes

pretty baby believe

pretty baby where were you

pretty baby look at me

pretty baby stay here

pretty baby—please

Maneater, A Warning

All women hustle

       tussle with muscle

searching for the next best thing

Even little girls

      who twirl their curls

look for Prince Charming

Sugar and spice

      at a nice price

we all know our power

We are equipped

With lips and hips

Women like me ***devour***

Words I Love

I love the word **bombshell**
Inamorata and **jezebel**
I enjoy saying **hellified**
When I'm dressed up and blow dried
I like the three syllables and the mouth feel
The way I say it closes the deal
I tell my husband he's **uxorious**
My **lexicon** is luxurious
Like shatoosh or cashmere
An expensive souvenir
Words like **raw** and **risk** make me smile
As do **elegant**, **quirk**, **freak** and **nubile**
I will use swear words as punctuation
Until the cuss police issue a citation
Motherfucker!--said with an exclamation
Dissolves every ounce of my frustration
A well placed word is a magical occurrence
Strong words are like weapons--my self defense

Words I Hate

I hate to be called **dear**
by men that I don't know
It's somewhat insincere
a wannabe Romeo

I despise the word **classy**
evadable and **cuckold**
I cringe when I'm called **sassy**
and disgruntled at **undersold**

Certain words are deal breakers
my affair with vocabulary
Reverse icebreakers
words like **nice** and **missionary**

With conversation...I'm mercenary
Sometimes I'd rather cuddle with my dictionary

Acrostic*

Obscenely expensive wine
Partake? I do, with pleasure
Unfair, really, that he has to work
So hard to provide these pretty bottles

Oblivious? I am, happily
Not concerned with the irony of
Enjoying this opulent buzz alone

*A poem or series of lines in which certain letters, usually the first in each line, form a name, motto, or message when read in sequence. For instance, the first letter of each line of this poem is highlighted. It reads 'Opus One.'

Peche

Je parle pour pécher
tous les jours
Il s'assied à ma table
pendant que je coupe les légumes pour le dîner
Il boit mon vin
et mange ma nourriture
qu'Il est à l'aise dans ma maison
j'apprécie sa compagnie

Translation:

Sin

I talk to sin
every day
He sits at my table
while I chop vegetables for dinner
He drinks my wine
and eats my food
He is comfortable in my house
I enjoy his company

Falling

I
drink
    drank
        drunk
and get
      crink
         crank
            crunk
then I
    sink
       sank
         sunk

Two Sides

She says:
We're friends
Platonic
He's not my boyfriend
He makes the perfect gin and tonic
I like talking to him on the phone
We enjoy each other's company
Just leave it alone

He says:
I wish we were friends
With benefits
She should be my girlfriend
I want to hit it
Her voice is sexy on the phone
Maybe I can get her drunk
I can't wait for us to be alone

Decadence

Daytime naps
Cashmere socks
Admirers, nightcaps
Massages while bumping Tupac
Wine at noon
Pedicures
Silver spoons
First edition literature
Nude photographs
Procrastination without consequence
Rowdy laughs
Making time for nonsense
Feeding whimsy
French lingerie
Languidly
Foreplay, fairways
Unapologetic
A decadent temptress offends
Skin and soft fabric
Her husband and boyfriend

Ode* to the Day Drunk

Some think of inebriation as a nighttime thing
Though some days require an adult beverage fling

Sometimes noon time is the witching hour
A pop of the cork dismisses willpower

It is five o'clock somewhere
Says the girl who enjoys a dare

The call of an intoxicant is strong
Seductive as a siren's song

Is drinking during daylight
Some sort of defense--like fight or flight?

To the nonbelievers I implore: Try it you'll like it
Just how much would be difficult to admit

Fuck tradition
There is power in submission

Sunshine drinking
Is for the free thinking

Drinking sunshine

Is beyond divine

*An ode is A lyric poem of some length, usually of a serious or meditative nature. My odes are hardly serious or meditative, though I still consider the poem above and the poem below to be odes.

Ode to Xanax

Written after a panic attack

The scrip warns not to operate
Heavy machinery
Why would I drive when my mind creates
Such fantastic scenery?

My love for Xanax
Is immeasurable
A tablet that rhymes with relax
Is so pleasurable

I'm not supposed to drink
When I take these pills
Booze and Xanax take me to the brink
The combination thrills

.25 milligrams
Is nifty

But God *damn*
.50

Would be a welcome increase
An invited shift
Time released
Extravagant gift

<u>Shopping</u>

Sometimes, when I
shop
at this little boutique in
STL
on Clayton Road   they open a bottle of
                             wine
                             for me to
                             sip
                             while I try on frocks
                             and blue jeans

Everyone knows my
name
even the new girls
Sipping, I sashay
in
and
out
of the dressing room   the salesladies remember
                             the girl I
                             was:
                             devastating, aloof--and they

marvel

at my accessibility now

We talk about hemlines and

tummy tucks

the wine tastes

crisp

like I am drinking

money

A Grown Man

He gives me tokens
Of his affection
Soft spoken
Adding to my collection
Glittery trinkets
His gifts make me glow
Forget
The boy I used to know
He makes time sprint
Sharing remember whens
Hints
Of back thens
A grown man
Solid, a boulder
My man
As I grow older

<u>Consonance*</u>

My mind trips
    A mental stutter
over pretty words and
poetic justice

Expressions slide
    Rich as butter
around my stumbling mind

An abundance
    Such clutter
old ideas
useless phrases
    flutter to the ground
    like litter

*consonance is the repetition of consonant sounds within words. In the above poem, the words stutter, butter,

clutter, flutter and litter are would be considered and example of consonance.

Fishing

There is an ocean

Between my ears

Full of words

Waiting to be caught

And cooked into poems

Iambic Pentameter

He wants me available and ready
Noticing secret, feminine details
Rewind, from behind, wicked and steady
Goddess he whispers *ultimate female*
Eight hundred count sheets protect like armor
A heated equation: flesh and cotton
Exposed but getting tender and warmer
Fear of the forbidden is forgotten
Who is this man who brings me such pleasure?
Elegant fingers, profane attraction
Craves and wants me more than he can measure
His obsession completes the transaction
Adoration and infatuation
Slower I whisper opening my eyes
His laugh is an erotic libation
Answered question, necessary sunrise

Exotic

written after reading Billy Collins

He tells me I'm exotic
and compares me to a sports car
A Lamborghini, he explains
not a Corvette. Too domestic.

His teeth: hypnotic
an orthodontists dream--five star
To make him smile again
What a bonus. His grin majestic.

His appeal: chaotic
mischief supreme--exemplar
We'd be wicked together, I maintain
A raw threat. That quick.

Hummingbird

There are many things
That I don't understand
Like math problems
The puzzle of quicksand

The suggestion
Of a question

In his iconic eyes
A futile exercise

That I struggle to solve
Evolve

Into the woman I was born to be
Where is the key

To this impossible lock?
Why is this clock

Running through time?
Does the answer lie in this useless rhyme?

Solutions: fleeting
A hummingbird
Exploring everything
Absurd!

Boredom

Most days, it feels like
a part of me drifts toward
the ceiling
to watch myself
have inane and shallow
conversations about
broken fingernails or
my most recent pedicure

As I float around different rooms
in different places
I watch myself fervently debate the
arch of my eyebrows and I feel so
tired
remembering dreams I once had
I don't remember saying that I wanted to
be a cliché when I grew up

I used to be an intellectual and
now all I can talk about
is my hair

Watching myself
detached
I realize that I have become
the type of woman
that I used to mock
before I got so tired and started
watching myself play
an endless game of pretend

Quincy

my home

tangible and dreamy

this land pulls me

toward contentment

laying on a rough blanket

of zoysia grass

I watch cottony clouds and

big sky

as my youngest son counts rocks

and my oldest climbs

an immense oak tree

this land is so flat

I feel I could

reach out

and

touch

the horizon

this town is my truth

More Whispers

lavish lines

luscious lies

these words are mine

a literal disguise

these lines

are lavish

luxurious and fine

my secret wish

rhymes divine

luscious

these lies

eternal and ageless

forever say yes

m e s m e r i z e

Acknowledgments:

Thank you to my husband, Dave, for understanding my poetic compulsion. Thank you also to my Father, Mohamed, my Mother, Zakiah, and my brother, Sayeed and his wife, Shelley. Our family brings me so much comfort.

Thank you to all my readers on Xanga , Blogger.com and MySpace. This book would never have been written if it wasn't for your constant feedback and encouragement. Carolyn Stevenson and Jill Tracy of Quincy, Richard Dix and C-Mac in St. Louis, Lance Powell in New York, Damon Marbury in Ohio, Ed Kaz, (America's favorite television editor ☺), Sheletha Manuel in North Carolina, Lolita Files in Los Angeles and Jennifer Croke in Denver ...your advice and constructive criticism means the world to me! Thank you.

Lisa Mason, from St. Louis, thank you, thank you not only for being a loyal reader of mine, but helping me decide on a title. We make a great team!

Last, but not least, Diane Dorce of Firefly Publishing— thank you for understanding my work and believing in me. Prom Queens Unite!

About the Author

Saadia Ali Aschemann lives in Quincy, Illinois with her husband and two sons. She is currently working towards her masters degree in educational leadership.